If You Meet a Dragon
and smaller challenges

TITLES IN THIS SET

Cover Artist
Petra Mathers was born in Germany. She
came to the United States and did odd jobs
so she could paint. She's written five books
and illustrated twelve. She loves it.

ISBN 0-673-80032-6

Copyright © 1993
Scott, Foresman and Company, Glenview, Illinois
All Rights Reserved.
Printed in the United States of America.

Acknowledgments appear on page 144.

2345678910 VHJ 9998979695949392

If You Meet a Dragon
and smaller challenges

INSTRUCTIONAL RESOURCE CENTER
Evergreen School District 114
2205 N.E. 138th Avenue
Vancouver, Washington 98684-7228

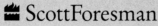

ScottForesman

A Division of HarperCollinsPublishers

Contents

That Wasn't So Bad

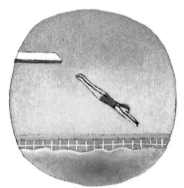

Meeting the Challenge
Genre Study

Everybody Is a Little Bit Different

Give It a Go!

CHIN CHIANG
AND THE
DRAGON'S DANCE

WRITTEN AND ILLUSTRATED BY
IAN WALLACE

From the time Chin Chiang stood only as high as his grandfather's knees, he had dreamed of dancing the dragon's dance. Now the first day of the Year of the Dragon had arrived and his dream was to come true. Tonight he would dance with his grandfather. But instead of being excited, Chin Chiang was so scared he wanted to melt into his shoes. He knew he could never dance well enough to make Grandfather proud of him.

He stopped sweeping the floor of his family's shop and looked into the street where his mother and father were busy with other shopkeepers, hanging up paper lanterns shaped like animals, fish and birds.

"It's time to practice our parts in the dragon's dance for the last time before the other dancers arrive, Chin Chiang. The afternoon is almost over," called Grandfather Wu from the bakeroom behind the shop.

"If I were a rabbit, I could run far away from here," Chin Chiang said to himself, "but then Mama, Papa and Grandfather really would be ashamed of me." So very slowly he walked into the bakeroom where Grandfather Wu stood waiting. He was wearing the splendid fierce dragon's head that he would put on again that night for the parade.

"Pick up the silk tail on the floor behind me," said his grandfather from inside the dragon's head, "and together we will be the most magnificent dragon that anyone has ever seen."

Chin Chiang did as he was asked, but as his grandfather started to dance, Chin Chiang did not move. "Grandfather can hide under the dragon's head," he whispered, "but if I trip or fall, I have nowhere to hide. Everyone will say, 'There goes clumsy Chin Chiang.' "

Grandfather Wu stopped dancing. "A dragon must have a tail as well as a head," he said gently.

Chin Chiang looked down at his shoes. "I can't dance the dragon's dance," he said.

"You have trained for a long time, Chin Chiang. Tonight, when you dance, you will bring tears of pride to your parents' eyes. Now come, join me and practice just as we have practiced before."

But when Chin Chiang tried to leap he tripped, stumbled and fell. Why had he ever thought he could dance the dragon's dance? Why had he ever wanted to? He was much too clumsy.

He jumped up and ran—away from his grandfather, out of the shop, into the market street. He stopped long enough to pick up a rabbit lantern, poke two holes for eyes and shove it over his head.

"Look, look. It's the dragon's tail!" called Mrs. Lau, dangling a speckled salmon for Chin Chiang to see. "Tonight, when you dance, the Great Dragon who lives in the clouds above the mountains will be honored, and next year he will fill our nets with beautiful fish like this."

Chin Chiang turned away.

"And he will grow oranges of a size and color never seen before," called Mr. Koo.

"What they say is true," added Mr. Sing. "The Great Dragon will bring prosperity and good fortune, if your dance pleases him."

But Chin Chiang remembered what one of the other dancers had once told him. If the dance was clumsy, the Great Dragon would be angry. Then he might toss the fruit from the trees and flood the valley. *It will all be my fault,* thought Chin Chiang. *Grandfather Wu will have to choose someone else to dance with him.* He waited to hear no more and raced across the market street.

"Our fish!" called Mrs. Lau.

"Our oranges!" called Mr. Koo.

Chin Chiang turned the corner.

"Our dance," called Grandfather Wu, from the doorway.

Looking out through the lantern, Chin Chiang hurried along the road by the sea to the public library, which he had visited many times when he wanted to be alone. He opened the door and ran up the stairs, round and round, higher and higher, up, up, up, to the door at the top that led out to the roof.

From his perch in the sky he could see the mountains rising above the sea and below him the animal lanterns, which would glow like tiny stars tonight. Chin Chiang felt happier than he had for many days.

"I never expected to meet a rabbit on top of this roof," called a strange voice.

Chin Chiang turned around quickly. A woman carrying a mop and pail was coming toward him.

"I'm not a rabbit," he said shyly. "I am Chin Chiang," and he pulled off the lantern.

"Oh, that is much better," she said. "Greetings, Chin Chiang. My name is Pu Yee. May I enjoy the view with you?" She didn't wait for a reply. "In a little while I'll be watching the New Year's parade from here. I used to dance the dragon's dance when I was young, but not any more. My feet are too old, and they are covered with corns."

"My grandfather dances the dragon's dance," said Chin Chiang, "and his corns are as old as yours."

Pu Yee laughed. "His old shoes may move his old bones, but my feet will never dance again."

A wonderful idea suddenly came to Chin Chiang. What if he had found someone to dance in his place? He would show Pu Yee his part in the dance right now. No one would see them if they tripped or fell. "You can help me practice what my grandfather taught me," he said.

"Oh, my creaky bones, what a funny sight that will be," said Pu Yee.

"You can dance," he told her. Cautiously Chin Chiang gave a little jump. Pu Yee jumped too. He shook slowly at first and she shook too. Next they leaped into the air, landed together and spun on their heels. Before long Pu Yee had forgotten her creaky bones. Then Chin Chiang stumbled and fell.

"Let's try again," said Pu Yee, picking him up.

While they danced, darkness had crept down slowly from the mountains to the city below. Then, from far off, Chin Chiang heard the lilting tune of pigeons with whistles tied to their tail feathers. They had been set free from their cages in the marketplace and were flying high above the buildings. Chin Chiang knew this meant that the New Year Festival had begun.

"We must go, Pu Yee. We're late," said Chin Chiang. "The pigeons are flying free."

"*I'm* not late," she replied. "I'm staying here."

But Chin Chiang pulled her by the hand, and they hurried down the stairs together—round and round, down, down, down, to the market street. The sound of firecrackers exploded in their ears while the eager crowd buzzed and hummed. Chin Chiang pushed his way forward, but Pu Yee pulled back. In the noise and confusion Chin Chiang let go of her hand, and suddenly he came face to face with the dragon whose head was wreathed in smoke.

"Where have you been, Chin Chiang? I have been sick with worry," called Grandfather Wu in a muffled voice. Chin Chiang did not reply. "Come now, take up the tail before the smoke disappears and everyone can see us."

Chin Chiang stood still, his feet frozen to the ground. The clamor of the street grew louder, stinging his ears. "I can't dance, Grandfather," he said.

Grandfather Wu turned away. "You can dance, Chin Chiang. Follow me."

"Look, look. Here comes the dragon!" called Mr. Sing. The crowd sent up a cheer that bounced off windows and doors and jumped into the sky.

Chin Chiang was trapped. Slowly he stooped and picked up the tail. Grandfather Wu shook the dragon's head fiercely until Chin Chiang started to kick up his heels to the beat of the thundering drum.

Then, suddenly, Chin Chiang stumbled, but instead of falling he did a quick step and recovered his balance. Excitedly, he leaped into the air, and again, and higher again. And as the dance went on, Chin Chiang's feet moved more surely, his steps grew firmer and his leaps more daring. Mrs. Lau and Mr. Koo cheered from their market shops while people poured out of their houses onto balconies and sidewalks, filling the streets. High in the sky flags of fire and falling moons burst into light. They sizzled and sparkled, rocketed straight up and whistled to the ground.

Just then Chin Chiang caught sight of a familiar face in the crowd. It was Pu Yee. Chin Chiang leaped to the sidewalk and pulled her into the street.

"I can't, Chin Chiang," she said, pulling away. "My bones. My corns. My knees."

"Pu Yee, yes, you can," Chin Chiang assured her. "Look at me!" Hesitantly she took hold of the tail and together they kicked up their heels just as they had on the rooftop, while the throngs of people cheered them on. Up one street and down another they danced, to the beat of the thundering drum.

All too soon the dragon lifted its head and shook its tail
for the last time. The dance was over. Pu Yee hugged
Chin Chiang close.

Grandfather Wu smiled inside the dragon's head. "Bring your
new friend to our home for dinner, Chin Chiang," he said. Pu Yee
and Chin Chiang hopped quickly over the doorstep and into the
bakeshop.

The family exchanged gifts of fine teas in wooden boxes, new
clothes and small red envelopes of Lucky Money. Then they sat
together to share plates of meat dumplings and carp, bowls
of steaming soup and trays of delicious pastries and cakes
and fresh fruit.

"To Chin Chiang, the very best dragon's tail I have ever seen,"
said Grandfather Wu, raising his glass in a toast.

Chin Chiang's face glowed with pride. "To a prosperous Year
of the Dragon," he said, raising his glass to his mama, papa,
grandfather and his new friend Pu Yee.

DRUM UP A DRAGON

by Ian Wallace

The first time I saw the dragon's dance, I was so impressed by it that I decided to tell a story about this Chinese tradition.

The morning dawned like so many other gray winter days. No blue moons while I slept and no double-yolked eggs at my breakfast to tell me I was about to discover my next book. There was just the raw cold that creeps about Toronto in February. It greeted me as I walked to work at the Art Gallery of Ontario.

Several hours later, however, a sign did appear. Not a sign I could see, but one I could hear. The beat of an ancient drum broke the quiet of my Sunday work place. The drum beat perked up my ears. It lured me away from my desk and out the gallery's front doors. Then I was rushing into the street to stand beside hundreds of other people lining the sidewalks. The excitement was electric!

In the center of the road was the most magnificent dragon I had ever seen. Its enormous, glittering head shook wildly to and fro. It rolled its eyes and flapped its jaws open and shut. Many dancing legs supported a brilliantly colored body of cloth scales. The twisting and curling and writhing breathed new life into the dragon and into the cold day. All around me lovely, glowing faces beamed their delight. *"Kung Hei Fat Choy!* Happy New Year!"

Looking around the excited crowd, I realized how important this tradition of the dancing dragon was for the Chinese. It was special for me, too. I knew then that I had to tell a story about this splendid dragon's dance.

THINKING
ABOUT IT

1. Think about what you have in common with Chin
    Chiang. Think about a time when you were afraid to
    try something. What do you remember? How did
    it turn out?

2. A Martian has just landed outside your school. He
    wants to know what Chinese New Year is like. What
    do you tell him?

3. Have you ever had a Chinese fortune cookie? A fortune
    cookie has a slip of paper baked inside with a wise
    saying or fortune on it. If Chin Chiang and Pu Yee each
    get a fortune cookie on the day of the New Year Festival,
    what will the fortunes say?

ANOTHER BOOK ABOUT FACING FEARS

Flip finds out that baseball takes practice and courage
in *Never Fear, Flip the Dip Is Here* by Philip Hanft.

BARBARA·SHOOK·HAZEN

The KNIGHT WHO WAS AFRAID OF THE DARK

PICTURES BY TONY·ROSS

Once long ago in a time known as the Dark Ages, there lived a bold and much loved knight. He was called Sir Fred.

He drove monsters out of the moat.

He chased the dishonest merchants out of town and saved the fair Lady Wendylyn from a hideous ten-headed dragon.

There was only one crack in Sir Fred's armor. Sir Fred was afraid—knee-bumping, heart-thumping afraid—of the dark.

He was afraid of the dark of the moon, the dark at
the top of the steep stone stairs, the dark at the bottom of
the big brass bed, and the dark between the head hole
and the arm hole when he put on his armor.

Because he was afraid, Sir Fred kept his bedchamber bright with candles. He kept a bottle of fireflies on his knight table and slept with his pet electric eel, whom he took with him if and when he had to get up to go to the bathroom.

Sir Fred was also afraid of being found out. Indeed there was one who suspected. That one was the castle bully, Melvin the Miffed.

Melvin the Miffed couldn't stand Sir Fred because he was better loved, especially by Lady Wendylyn.

Melvin the Miffed stalked the castle corridors, sneaking and peeking and trying to find the crack in Sir Fred's armor.

Melvin the Miffed observed that Sir Fred did all his brave deeds in broad daylight. All the other knights liked the cover of darkness.

He also saw that Sir Fred was the only knight who did *not* cower under the Round Table during thunder and lightning storms.

Indeed, the bolder the bolt, the better.

Moreover he observed that Sir Fred only met Lady
Wendylyn on nights when the moon was full, which was
why they seldom saw each other and why Lady Wendylyn
began to wonder if she was truly Sir Fred's True Love.

Things came to a head one dark day when Melvin the Miffed sneaked up and peeked at a letter Lady Wendylyn was reading.

"If your True Love truly wanted to see you," Melvin the Miffed whispered, "he wouldn't make up silly excuses not to."

"Wicked good point," Lady Wendylyn said, tossing her curls and stamping her foot.

That afternoon Lady Wendylyn embroidered a banner and hung it out her window.

Sir Fred saw the banner and sank into deep despair.

The evening sky was exceedingly dark and the moon was thin as a mouse's whisker. Sir Fred pummeled his pillow and hemmed and hawed, "Oh, woe, shall I stay? Or shall I go?

"If I don't go, I will lose my ladylove because she will think I don't love her. If I do go, I will lose my ladylove because she will think I am scared of the dark, which I am."

In the end Sir Fred went. His fear was big. But so was his love. He went armed with a fistful of fireflies, a glowworm-studded shield, and his faithful electric eel wound around his arm.

Lady Wendylyn was waiting by the fountain with her eyes tightly closed. At the stroke of midnight she opened them and shrieked, "EEEEEEEEEEEEEEEEEEEEEEK!"

As she shrieked, she grabbed Sir Fred's hands, released
the fireflies, flung the shield to the ground, and tweaked the
electric eel's tail light, leaving Sir Fred terrified in total
darkness.

"EEEEEEEEEEEEEEK! Get off my True Love!" Lady
Wendylyn shrieked again as she flicked a last lingering
firefly from Sir Fred's sleeve.

"To tell the truth," she then said, "I'm terrified of bugs and all slithery things that creep and crawl."

Sir Fred then did his bravest deed. He told Lady Wendylyn the truth about himself. "I am," he admitted, "afraid of the dark—knee-bumping, heart-thumping afraid—of the dark."

"Then you are even braver than I thought," Lady
Wendylyn said, flinging her arms around Sir Fred, "because
you met me anyway."

"And you are brave as well as beautiful," Sir Fred said
with a kiss, "because you tried to protect me."

Melvin the Miffed was still sneaking and peeking around.

He saw the loving scene and snorted, "How sickening!"
Then he stamped his feet and stalked off forever.

Nobody saw him leave. Lady Wendylyn was too busy
patting Sir Fred's electric eel and saying, "Hmmm, he's not
as scary as I thought."

Meanwhile Sir Fred was clutching his True Love and
telling her, "Hmmm, the dark's not so scary either.
With someone."

THINKING ABOUT IT

1. Sir Fred is afraid of the dark. Lady Wendylyn doesn't like spiders. What fears of your own did you think of as you read the story? How do you keep from being afraid?

2. Sir Fred used many things to feel safe in the dark. What were they? Which one worked best?

3. DRAGON! The knights have to rush into the darkness to fight the dragon. What will Sir Fred do? How can he keep from feeling scared?

The Diver

by ALEXANDER RESNIKOFF

This time I'll do it! Mommy, look!
I promise I won't be a fool—
I'm going to climb on that diving board
And dive right into the pool!

Look at me, Mom; I'm doing it!
I never have done it before—
I'm climbing those steps to the diving board.
I'll count them: One, two, three, four. . . .

Look, Mom! I'm on the diving board!
This carpet feels terribly rough—
It hurts the tan on the soles of my feet,
But I can take it; I'm tough.

And now I'm jumping up and down
Right by the steps—Mommy, look!
You sure you're looking? Saw me jump?
Now *please,* Mommy, put down that book!

Hey, Mom, I'm going farther now—
It's cold here; I'm starting to shake,
But I go forward, inch by inch—
I hope these boards will not break.

Look at me, Mom! I'm at the end!
I must be a thousand feet high!
Or maybe higher—I'm not sure
I'm looking with only one eye.

I'll say a prayer, I'll take a deep breath,
I'll hold my nose, and I'll plop—
Maybe you should move a little way back—
Those waves might go over the top!

Mom, are you looking? Watch me
I hope that you are prepared—
Look at me, Mommy, here I come
One . . .
Two . . .
Three . . .
. . . .
. . . .
I am scared. . . .

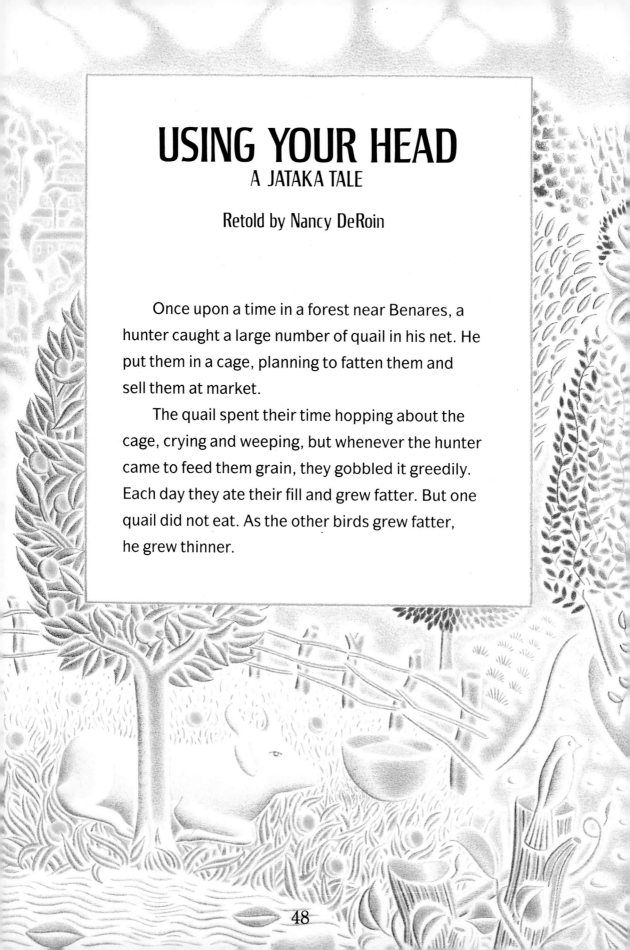

USING YOUR HEAD
A JATAKA TALE

Retold by Nancy DeRoin

Once upon a time in a forest near Benares, a hunter caught a large number of quail in his net. He put them in a cage, planning to fatten them and sell them at market.

The quail spent their time hopping about the cage, crying and weeping, but whenever the hunter came to feed them grain, they gobbled it greedily. Each day they ate their fill and grew fatter. But one quail did not eat. As the other birds grew fatter, he grew thinner.

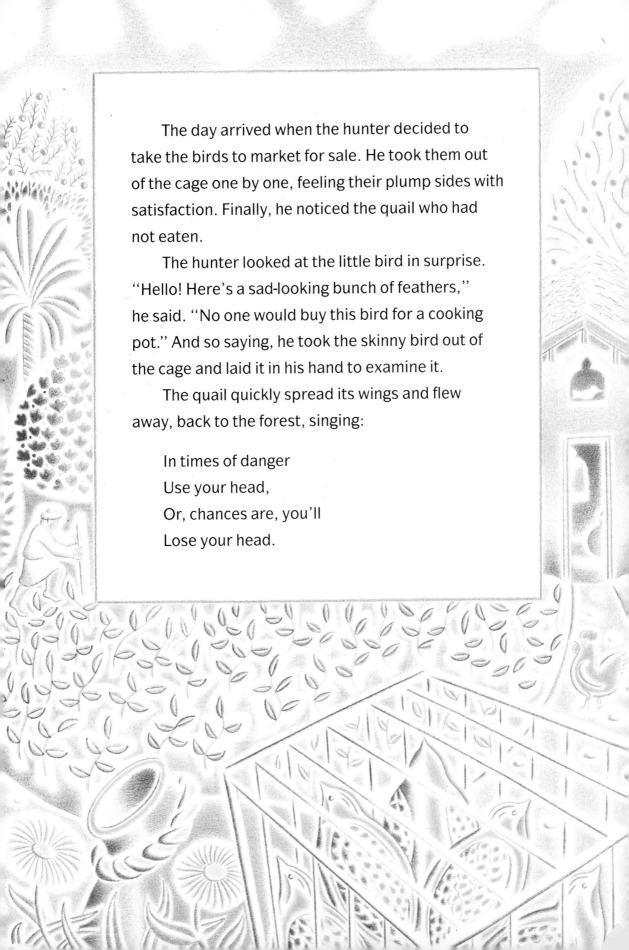

The day arrived when the hunter decided to take the birds to market for sale. He took them out of the cage one by one, feeling their plump sides with satisfaction. Finally, he noticed the quail who had not eaten.

The hunter looked at the little bird in surprise. "Hello! Here's a sad-looking bunch of feathers," he said. "No one would buy this bird for a cooking pot." And so saying, he took the skinny bird out of the cage and laid it in his hand to examine it.

The quail quickly spread its wings and flew away, back to the forest, singing:

In times of danger
Use your head,
Or, chances are, you'll
Lose your head.

The Tiger and the Fox

When the tiger was out hunting one day deep in the forest, he caught a fox.

As he prepared to eat his prey; the fox said to the tiger, "You must not eat me. I am the king of the forest. Come with me and I will show you how the other animals fear me."

狐假虎威

a Chinese fable retold and illustrated by Demi

When the other animals saw the big tiger following the fox, they scattered in many different directions.

"I see what you mean," said the tiger, not realizing it was from him, not the fox, that the animals were fleeing. "I'd better find something else to eat."

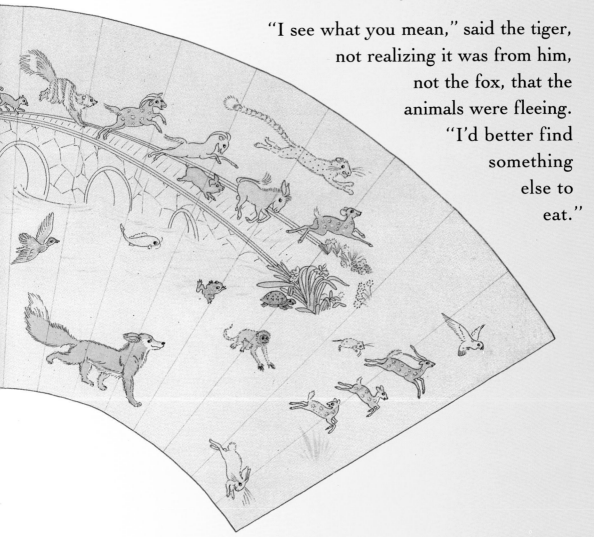

Small creatures must live by their wits.

The Fox and the Goat

an Aesop's fable retold by Anne Terry White

One day a Fox was nosing around a well. By bad luck his foot slipped on a wet stone and he fell in. The water wasn't deep, but the well was. And though he wore himself out trying to get out, the Fox could not do it.

"What in the world are you doing down there in the well?" he heard someone ask. He looked up. There stood a Goat peering down in the well.

The Fox's spirits rose. He saw hope ahead.

"Enjoying myself!" he replied. "They say there will be no rain for a long time and all the wells will go dry. So I am drinking my fill before it happens. Come on down—the water's fine."

The foolish Goat didn't stop to think. He jumped right in.

The Fox, of course, wanted to use him for a ladder and leaped at once on the Goat's back. Then he set one foot on his horns and jumped out of the well.

"Good-by, my friend," he called out from above. "And next time, silly Goat, look before you leap!"

Think how you will get out before you get in.

DOCTOR COYOTE

a Native American Aesop's fable

RETOLD BY **JOHN BIERHORST**

Traveling along, Coyote met White Beard, and the two of them traveled together.

When Coyote and White Beard got thirsty, they jumped into a well. They drank their fill. Then White Beard began looking around to see how he could get back out.

"Don't worry," said Coyote. "I know how we can do it. Just stand up straight and put your hands against the side of the well. Lift your head so your horns stick out behind, and I'll climb on your back. As soon as I'm out, I'll reach over and pull you up."

It sounded good to White Beard. He did what he was told, and Coyote climbed on top of him. But then, when Coyote was free, he ran around the edge of the well, laughing at White Beard. White Beard was furious.

"Friend," said Coyote, "if your brain was as big as your beard, you would have thought about how to get out before you jumped in."

The truth hits hardest when it's too late to complain.

THINKING ABOUT IT

1. Such silly, tricky, and wise animals! Which one is most like you? How are the two of you alike?

2. Fables teach a lesson. Fables have action. Fables often have animals. Which fable that you read will you use to tell someone what a fable is? How will you tell them? How will you show them?

3. You've been in school for a few years now and you're a pro. What moral would you want beginners to learn about school? Make up a fable to teach your moral.

MORE ABOUT DOCTOR COYOTE

That trickster Doctor Coyote continues to teach us lessons in *Doctor Coyote: A Native American Aesop's Fables* retold by John Bierhorst.

City Mouse and Country Mouse

a play by Jane Buxton based on Aesop's fable

C H A R A C T E R S

CITY MOUSE (dressed in trendy clothes)

COUNTRY MOUSE (dressed in overalls and gumboots)

DOG **FIRST CAT** **SECOND CAT**

S C E N E 1

COUNTRY MOUSE *stands outside a mousehole in the country.* CITY MOUSE *comes in, carrying a suitcase.*

CITY MOUSE Hi there, country cousin! Very kind of you to invite me for a holiday. I've never been to the country.

COUNTRY MOUSE You're welcome, Cousin City Mouse.

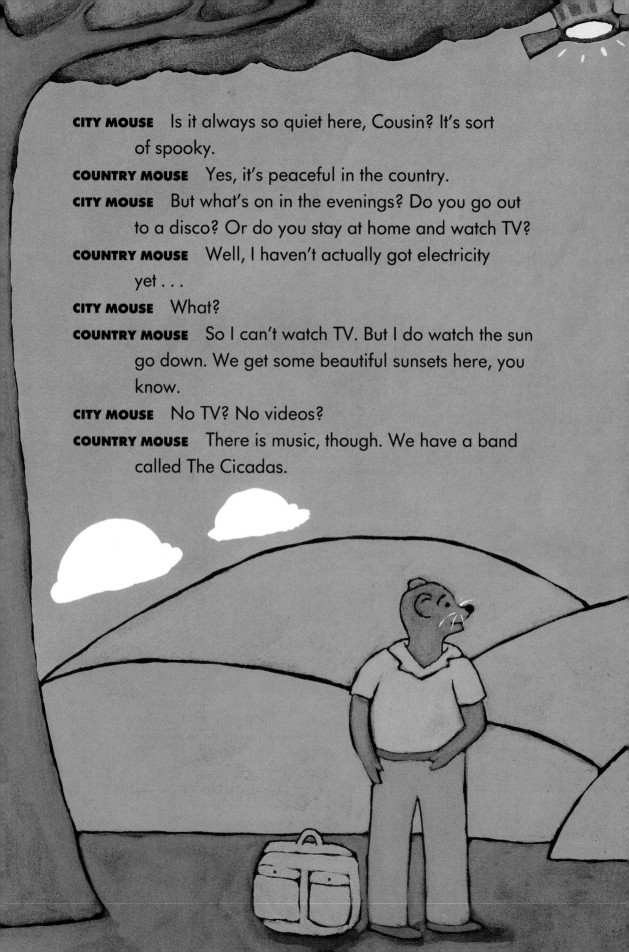

CITY MOUSE   Is it always so quiet here, Cousin? It's sort of spooky.

COUNTRY MOUSE   Yes, it's peaceful in the country.

CITY MOUSE   But what's on in the evenings? Do you go out to a disco? Or do you stay at home and watch TV?

COUNTRY MOUSE   Well, I haven't actually got electricity yet . . .

CITY MOUSE   What?

COUNTRY MOUSE   So I can't watch TV. But I do watch the sun go down. We get some beautiful sunsets here, you know.

CITY MOUSE   No TV? No videos?

COUNTRY MOUSE   There is music, though. We have a band called The Cicadas.

CITY MOUSE Cicadas? Never heard of them. Hey, Cousin, I'm hungry. What's for lunch?

COUNTRY MOUSE Well, I can offer you . . . .

CITY MOUSE You haven't got any pizzas, have you? Back home I hang out in a pizza parlor. I can really pig out there. Believe me, Cousin, a pizza parlor's a cool spot for a mouse.

COUNTRY MOUSE I'm afraid I don't have anything like that. But here's a freshly picked ear of wheat and some acorns. If you're still hungry, I can get you some fine windfall apples.

CITY MOUSE Sorry, I'm not really into health foods. Look, this holiday isn't going to work out. I suppose tonight you'll expect me to watch a good old-fashioned sunset with you.

COUNTRY MOUSE   Well . . . I . . . er . . .

CITY MOUSE   I thought as much. I don't want to be rude, Cousin, but don't you think it's a little *boring* here?

COUNTRY MOUSE   Is it? Well, perhaps it is . . . I've never thought about it. What's it like in the city?

CITY MOUSE   It's cool, mouse. There's always something on in the city. But the best thing is the food—pizzas, crisps, fizzy drink, ice-cream . . .

COUNTRY MOUSE   It sounds too good to be true.

CITY MOUSE   Well, it's not too late. We could go now.

COUNTRY MOUSE   Now? To the city?

CITY MOUSE   Sure. Why not? I don't think I could spend the night here. It's so quiet I wouldn't get to sleep.

COUNTRY MOUSE   All right I *will* go to the city with you. I'd certainly like to try some of that delicious food.

CITY MOUSE   Cool, mouse! Let's go!

(They both leave.)

SCENE 2

Outside a mousehole under a table in the city. Loud music. Flashing lights. CITY MOUSE *pulls up an empty cigarette packet for* COUNTRY MOUSE *to sit on. Music fades.*

CITY MOUSE   Have a seat, Cousin.

COUNTRY MOUSE   Thank you. Nice place you have here. Will it be dinner time soon?

CITY MOUSE   Sure will. This is called a birthday party. *(A large human foot descends beside them.)* Watch out!

COUNTRY MOUSE   *(jumping up)* Yikes! What's that? *(The foot moves away.)*

CITY MOUSE That was a human foot. Have to watch out for them. Here's some food dropping now. Crackers and cheese. Help yourself. Be my guest.

COUNTRY MOUSE Why, thank you, Cousin. It looks delicious.
(*Enter* DOG.)

DOG Woof, woof, woof!

CITY MOUSE Quick! Quick! Into the hole.
(*Both* MICE *run into the hole and peep out as the dog runs off.*)

COUNTRY MOUSE (*trembling*) My, that was close.

CITY MOUSE (*shrugging*) You get used to it.
(*Both* MICE *come out and sit under the table again. Some salami drops from the table.* CITY MOUSE *picks it up and gives it to* COUNTRY MOUSE.)

CITY MOUSE Have some salami. Now this is *real* food. Beats acorns any day, don't you think?

COUNTRY MOUSE What's it made of?

CITY MOUSE Cats!

(He runs into the mousehole.)

COUNTRY MOUSE *(looking at salami in horror)* Cats?

(He drops the salami.)

CITY MOUSE No, you nerd. The cats are coming!

(He reaches out and pulls COUNTRY MOUSE *into the hole just as the cats enter.)*

FIRST CAT Meow. I smell mice.

SECOND CAT Meyum, yum. I smell salami.

*(*CATS *share salami and leave.* CITY MOUSE *comes out of the hole, dragging* COUNTRY MOUSE *behind him.)*

CITY MOUSE Drat those cats. They've eaten our salami.

COUNTRY MOUSE *(trembling)* At least they haven't eaten us.

CITY MOUSE Don't be a wimp, Cousin Country Mouse. Live dangerously. Have some fun while you're in the city. Ah, look! There's a spilt glass of something or other.

COUNTRY MOUSE Ooh, I've never tasted Something or Other before.

(Both MICE *creep closer. A human hand reaches out for the glass.)*

CITY MOUSE Run for it!

COUNTRY MOUSE Help!

(They run to the mousehole. Music begins—the Happy Birthday song.)

CITY MOUSE   Cool, mouse, cool! They're playing the cake music. Wait till you taste the cake! And icing! And candles! Delicious!

COUNTRY MOUSE   I'll take your word for it, Cousin City Mouse. But I'm not staying for the cake.

CITY MOUSE   You won't stay?

COUNTRY MOUSE   No. I've just remembered something I have to do back home. Goodbye and thank you.

CITY MOUSE   Well, goodbye, Cousin. I hope you enjoyed city life. But what have you suddenly remembered?

COUNTRY MOUSE   I've remembered how I can take off my boots and relax when I'm in the country. If I hurry home, I'll be just in time to sit by my front door and watch the sunset. Goodbye!

Thinking About It

1. In this play, you see two very different places to live. Which one would you choose—city or country? How would you get a friend to visit you in your new home?
2. This fable is set in modern times. What clues in the play tell us this?
3. A play needs scenery and costumes. You are in charge of the play. What will your scenery look like? What will your actors wear?

Manhattan Lullabye

BY NORMA FARBER

Lulled by rumble, babble, beep,
let these little children sleep;
let these city girls and boys
dream a music in the noise,
hear a tune their city plucks
up from buses, up from trucks
up from engines wailing *fire!*
up ten stories high, and higher,
up from hammers, rivets, drills,
up tall buildings, over sills,
up where city children sleep,
lulled by rumble, babble, beep.

Country Road, Spring Walk

BY FRANK ASCH

Roll up the moon,
raise the sun,
time for a change of scene.
Look at a rose,
swim in its red.
Have you ever seen
such a green?
Holes in my socks,
toes in my holes,
as plain as the day
on your face.
Dew in the grass,
sun in the dew,
shining all
over the place.

THINKING BIG

THE STORY OF A YOUNG DWARF

text and photographs
by Susan Kuklin

Wherever Jaime Osborn goes, she stands out. When her parents take her places, people stare. Sometimes they come up to her and pat her on the head as if she were a puppy. Strangers ask her questions like, "How old are you?" Jaime says, "I'm eight." Generally, she can guess what's coming next. If they know how big an average eight-year-old is, they might ask, "Are you a midget?"

Jaime doesn't mind explaining why she is so small. "My limbs did not grow as long as other people's," she says, "because I'm a dwarf. Dwarfs are supposed to be small." Most people don't understand that a midget is short all over, while a dwarf like Jaime has short arms and legs on an average-size body.

Jaime's brother, Matthew, is five years old. He is not a dwarf and is much taller than his big sister. Most dwarfs have average-size parents, brothers, and sisters in their families. Matthew says, "I love my sister. She is a very good sister. I like her as a dwarf. It doesn't matter what she is."

Jaime likes it that Matthew is bigger because he can do some favors for her. When she sold Girl Scout Cookies, for example, she took Matthew along. "I'm a good seller," she says. "People can't say no, but first I have to get them to open their doors. That's where Matthew comes in. I can't reach the doorbells. He does it for me."

Jaime also does favors for Matthew. Her brother is only five and cannot read. But Jaime is an excellent reader. Matthew loves having a smart, big sister to play with and to teach him numbers and the ABC's.

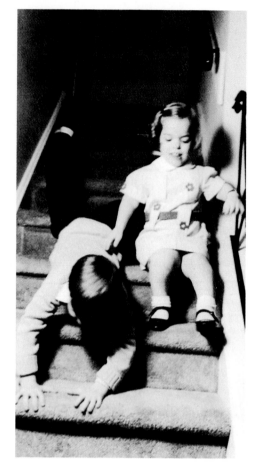

To Jaime, it often seems as if the world were built for giants. Every morning, when she and Matthew go downstairs for breakfast, Jaime has to go down the steps differently than other eight-year-olds. Imagine what it would be like to walk up and down stairs that hit you at the knee. That's what it's like for Jaime. Going up means hiking one foot as high as her other knee, shifting her body from one side to the other, and pulling herself up. Coming down is much easier. She sits and slides to the bottom.

When they are downstairs, if their parents aren't up, Matthew and Jaime make their own breakfast. Jaime can reach only as high as the second shelf of the refrigerator. The milk and jelly are higher, so Matthew gets them for her. If Matthew isn't nearby, she just kicks off her shoes and climbs into the refrigerator to get them herself. But she must move fast. Her feet get cold.

Before she goes out, Jaime sits patiently while her mother curls her hair. "I like looking pretty," says Jaime.

On school days, Jaime's mother puts her on the bus. She lifts her up to the top of the steps. At first, when Jaime left the bus, she would sit down and bounce down the steps. The driver complained that this wasn't safe. So now, even though she would prefer getting off the bus by herself, one of her friends holds her hand and helps her.

"Hi, this is your lucky day. You've just met your first dwarf!" Jaime told Lamont when they met. Lamont is the smartest boy in the whole third grade. He's also the tallest. Lamont and Jaime are best buddies.

When Jaime sits at her desk, her feet, unlike the other children's, do not touch the ground. For a long time she let them dangle in midair, but they would fall asleep. That hurt. Then her mother brought a stool to place under the desk. Now Jaime can rest her feet and not worry about them.

Jaime has a special team of friends who sit with her at the number one reading table. When the teacher asks a question, Jaime's hand usually shoots up first. She loves to read out loud or answer the teacher's questions. Jaime is never shy when it comes to speaking out. Even the teacher agrees that Jaime has the loudest voice in the whole class.

With such short legs holding up her average-size body, it is hard for Jaime to stand or walk for a long time. When she goes on hikes with her class, the other children usually get way ahead. Sometimes, when Jaime runs to catch up, she loses her balance and falls forward. Jaime falls a lot, but she never cries.

Although Jaime wants to be treated just like everyone else, that's not always possible. In gym, she must wear knee pads because her joints are not as strong as other children's. Grandma Mimi made special ones for her. They say "Big J.O." Lamont helps Jaime in gym, especially when they play basketball.

One subject in which Jaime needs no help is art. She is so good that her classmates come to her for help with their drawings. In fact, Jaime says she may become an artist when she grows up. In art, Jaime sits with her team, her best girlfriends from her reading group.

During lunch recess, Jaime likes to ride the small seesaw with her friends. "Sometimes they want to go on the big one," she says, "and I can't play on it. So I go somewhere by myself." Everyone cannot always do small-scale things. Jaime knows that.

"The kindergarteners can be nasty," Jaime recalls. "They may call me names. They say, 'Look at that little baby, look at that little baby.' I tell them that I'm *not* a baby. I'm supposed to be little. I'm a dwarf. If they don't pay attention to what I tell them, I just ignore them. Besides, everybody is a little bit different." Once Jaime's teacher asked her if the children hurt her feelings. She said, "No way . . . no, ma'am!" Jaime is proud of who she is.

THINKING ABOUT IT

1. Jaime lives near you. What do you do together? How do you help each other?

2. We're all different and sometimes we're curious about each other's differences. What questions would you like to ask Jaime?

3. What kind of home would be perfect for Jaime? What could be in it to make her life easier?

ANOTHER BOOK ABOUT CHALLENGES

Margaret may be in a wheelchair, but she's going to find a way to outrun her brothers in *Margaret's Moves* by Berniece Rabe.

The Boy and the Ghost

by Robert D. San Souci / illustrations by J. Brian Pinkney

Down south, there was once a boy named Thomas whose family was very poor. His parents worked hard from sunup to sundown on their little backcountry farm, but could barely put enough food on the table to feed their seven children. Thomas had two brothers and a sister older than he was, and two sisters and a brother who were younger, so he was right smack in the middle.

Because he hated to see his parents work so hard, and his brothers and sisters go hungry all the time, the boy made up his mind to go to the city to earn some money, so he could bring it back and help his family.

Since the older children had to help their parents chop cotton, and the younger ones were too little to go off on their own, Thomas, in the middle, decided *he* ought to be the one to try and help in this way.

He set out the next morning. His mother hugged him and gave him a pot and a hambone to make soup and said, "Now, you always be polite to anyone you meet, and generous as well."

Then his father embraced the boy, gave him a box of matches and a croaker-sack to carry things in, and told Thomas, "Be brave, no matter what happens, and always be honest."

"We'll miss you!" cried his three sisters and three brothers, and they hugged him one and all.

"I'll miss you, too," said Thomas, putting on a brave smile to hide how sad he felt at leaving. So, off he went.

As he walked along the road that led to the city, he picked up sticks for a fire. And he found some greens and other good things that grew wild, and put these in his croaker-sack.

When he stopped for lunch, he lit a fire. Then he filled his pot with fresh water from a stream and added the hambone and the things he had gathered. Soon he had some soup boiling away nicely.

When he was ready to eat, a poor man came by, even more raggedy than Thomas, and asked, "Can I have just a taste of that soup?"

"Of course," said the little boy, politely inviting the raggedy man to dip his tin cup into the broth. Together, they finished the soup, and tasty it was.

When they were done, the man said, "Where're you heading, boy?"

"To the city to earn money so's I can help my family," he answered.

"You mightn't have to go so far," said the other, "if you're brave enough.

"I hear there's a house on a hill not far from here. A rich man lived there years ago, but he died. Folks say the place's haunted. But the same folks say anyone who stays in it from sunset to sunrise will get the house and the treasure the old man hid before he died."

"Why don't you go and get the treasure yourself?" Thomas asked.

"I'm scared—that's the long 'n' short of it. Folks say everyone who's tried to last the night has run away or died of fright. Now, no one'll go near the place."

Thomas thought of his poor family at home.

"*I will*," he said, gathering up his hambone and pot, and putting them in his croaker-sack.

Soon after, boy and man parted company. Just before sunset, Thomas spotted the lonely old house on the hill.

Bravely, he walked up and pushed open the door with a *Scriiiitch!*

Inside, most of the dusty rooms and cobwebby hallways were empty. But, in the kitchen, he found a big old iron stove opposite a fireplace. There were also a table with one chair, a candle and a spoon.

The boy lit the candle. Then he put the last of his kindling in the stove, drew some water from a well outside the back door, and put in the hambone and remaining greens to make soup for his supper.

While it was warming, a bright light suddenly filled the fireplace across the room. There was an awful moan. Then a thin, sad voice wailed down the chimney, "Look out, my legs are falling!"

With a *Whoomp!* a pair of legs encased in elegant trousers, starting at fine leather shoes and ending at a wide belt with a gold buckle, dropped into the ashes in the cold fireplace.

Immediately, they got up and began running around the kitchen. They kicked at walls and doors and even the side of the big iron stove, so Thomas had to keep moving out of their way.

"Aren't you going to run away?" asked the ghostly voice.

"I'm fine right where I am, just so's you don't kick over my soup," Thomas said, stirring the boiling pot.

Just as he was ready to carry his soup to the table, the voice wailed down the chimney, "Look out, my arms are falling!"

And, with a *Whump!* a man's two arms and middle, clothed in a silken shirt with silver buttons, dropped into the fireplace. Immediately, the legs went over and stood waiting, while the other part climbed up and settled in place. Then the headless body fumbled around the kitchen, rattling cupboards and pounding on walls.

"Aren't you going to run away?" the strange voice
called down the chimney.

But Thomas, who was sitting at the table, dipping up
his broth with the spoon, answered, "No need to. Just
see that you don't knock over my soup."

"Look out!" warned the voice, "Here comes the rest
of me!"

Then a scowling head, with hair and beard red as flame
and eyes like blazing coals, dropped *Thunk!* into the
fireplace ashes.

Right away the body of the man, or ghost, or whatever
it was, picked up the head from the hearth, brushed it
off, and set it squarely on its shoulders.

"Now," roared the figure, hands on hips, "what do
you say?"

"Do you want some soup?" asked Thomas, who
wouldn't let his courage or his manners fail him. "There's
still a little left in the pot, and you're welcome to share it."

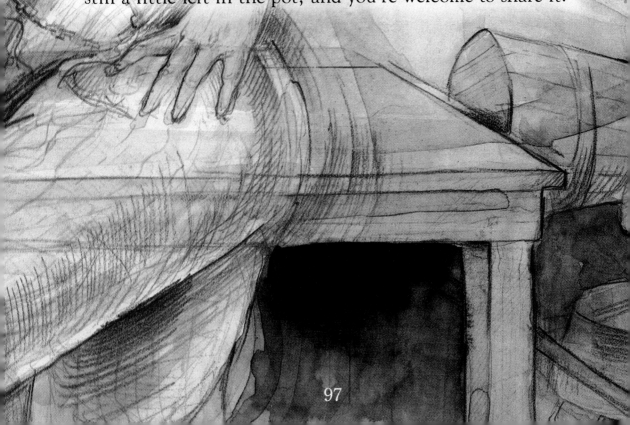

The ghostly figure said, "I don't need any food. But you're the only one, man or boy, who's stayed long enough for me to put myself together. Now, follow me." He raised his left hand. Immediately, his fingers blazed like a torch, though the fire didn't seem to hurt him any. "Now fetch the shovel that's out by the well, and follow me—if you dare!"

"I will," said Thomas.

The ghost led the little boy to a lonely spot far from the house. Stopping under a huge sycamore tree, the ghost pointed with his right hand to the ground near its roots. "Dig there," he commanded.

Thomas dug and dug, until the shovel fell from his blistered hands. The ghost remained silent, one hand raised and glowing, the finger of his other hand still pointing to the hole.

After a short rest, Thomas wearily began digging again. Soon the point of his shovel struck something hard. He uncovered a large earthen pot caked with dirt. When he lifted the lid, he saw gold and silver coins shining in the first glow of sunrise.

"Give half my money to the poor, so my soul can rest easy," said the ghost, as his legs faded away, "and keep half for yourself." His arms and middle disappeared up to his neck.

"You're a good, brave lad," added the floating head, with a wink. "You set me free, and I thank you."

"You're—" Thomas began, but the head was gone before he could say,—"welcome."

Thomas did as he was told. He loaded the gold and silver into his croaker-sack. On his way home, he gave half the money away to poor folk.

When he got back to the farm, his family was overjoyed to have him back safe and sound. Then the boy shared his wealth with the rest of his family, and they all moved into the house on the hill and lived happily ever after. And the ghost was never seen again in those parts.

Thinking About It

1. "Whoomp! First the legs dropped into the ashes of the cold fireplace." You're in the kitchen with Thomas. How do you act as the ghost appears to you bit by bit?

2. "You're a good, brave lad," says the ghost to Thomas. Do you agree with the ghost? Give your reasons.

3. What a mystery! Who was the ghost? Why was he trapped in the lonely house on the hill? Where did he get all that money? Explain the ghost's past.

IF YOU SAY SO, CLAUDE

BY
Joan Lowery Nixon

ILLUSTRATIONS BY
Lorinda Bryan Cauley

CHAPTER

1

In the spring, after the last of the big snows, Shirley and Claude drove down from the silver-mining towns of the Rocky Mountains. They headed for that great state called Texas.

Claude was as short as he was broad, with a curly gray beard that waggled when he talked. Shirley was as tall as a doorpost, and almost as thin, with hair and skin the color of prairie dust with the sun on it. They drove in a covered wagon pulled by two sway-backed, but good-natured, horses.

"I can't abide those minin' towns any longer, Shirley," Claude said. "All that shootin' and yellin' is too rough a life for me. I've heard there's plenty of peace and quiet to be found in that great state called Texas."

"If you say so, Claude," Shirley said. But she missed the mountains and the forests and the plumb good looks of the Colorado Territory.

They followed a trail that cut south and turned
east into upper West Texas, where long canyons dug
deep into the hard rock.

"Will you look at that!" Claude cried. He eased
the horses and wagon down a trail to the bottom of a
narrow, rocky canyon. The purple shadows lay over
them, and the silence lay around them.

"Shirley, I do believe this is the peaceful place
we've been lookin' for," Claude said.

"I hope not," Shirley said. "I don't really take to
this place, Claude. I feel like I'm in a four-sided box."

"Never mind. This land will grow on you,
Shirley," Claude said. "For now, why don't you take
the rifle and see if you can hunt up some meat for the
table. I'll get our sleepin' pallets out of the wagon and
tend to the horses."

So Shirley unfolded her long legs, stuck her feet in her boots, hiked up her skirts, and climbed down from the wagon. She took the rifle and edged past the back of the wagon. Right off she spied a fat, lop-eared rabbit sitting on a rock ledge just across the narrow canyon; so she raised the rifle and fired.

Shirley's aim never was very good, so she missed the rabbit; and that old bullet bounced off the rock and back and forth across the canyon, whanging and banging, zinging and zanging, making a terrible racket. Shirley and the rabbit just froze, staring wide-eyed at each other.

Well, Claude took that moment to stick his head out the back of the wagon to see what that awful noise was, and the bullet tore right through the top of his hat, dropping it in the dust at Shirley's feet.

Claude looked across the canyon just in time to see the rabbit hightail it behind the ledge. He thought on it for a moment. Then he said, "Shirley, get back in the wagon. I don't think we want to live in a place where we can't go out to get meat for the table without the rabbits shootin' back. We're gonna have to move on."

Shirley picked up Claude's hat, climbed back into the wagon, and gave a happy sigh of relief.

"If you say so, Claude," she said.

CHAPTER

2

For two days Shirley and Claude headed south, farther down into that great state called Texas. The sun was mean enough to sizzle lizards and curl up the cracks in the dried-out earth, when Claude pulled the sweating, but good-natured, horses to a stop.

He said, "Shirley, I do believe this is the peaceful place we've been lookin' for."

Shirley gazed at the flat landscape that stretched before her gray and bleak, broken only by clumps of scrubby mesquite. And she said, "I hope not, Claude. This land has got the worst case of the uglies I've ever seen."

"Never mind. It'll grow on you, Shirley," Claude said. "For now, why don't you go see what you can find in the way of firewood. I'll get our sleepin' pallets out of the wagon and tend to the horses."

So Shirley unfolded her long legs, stuck her feet
in her boots, hiked up her skirts, and climbed down
from the wagon. She walked back aways, among the
clumps of mesquite. Suddenly she heard an angry
rattle. She looked down, and her right boot was
planted square on the neck of a mad five-foot
diamondback rattler that had stretched out in the
shade to take a nap.

Before she could think what to do, she heard
another noise. She looked over to her left to see a
mean little wild hog. Its beady eyes glared, its sharp
tusks quivered, and its small hooves pawed the
ground, getting ready to charge.

Quick as she could, Shirley stooped down, grabbed the snake careful like around the neck, and, using it as a whip, flipped its tail at the wild hog. That tail, rattle and all, wrapped itself tight about the neck of the hog.

But the hog was coming fast, and all Shirley could do was hang onto the snake and use all her strength to twirl the hog clear off his feet and round and around her head. With a zap she let go. The snake fell to the ground, done for. But the hog flew off, squealing and snorting and carrying on something awful.

Shirley's aim never was very good, so it happened that just as Claude climbed down from the wagon to see what was making the terrible racket, that hog sailed right past his face, nearly brushing the end of his nose.

Claude watched the hog until he was out of sight, way yonder past a far clump of mesquite, and he thought on it for a moment.

"Shirley," he called, "get back in the wagon. It seems to me a man has a right to set foot outside his wagon without gettin' bad-mouthed by a wild hog who wants the right of way. Especially," he added, "when that hog's in a place no hog ever ought to be. We're gonna have to move on."

Shirley climbed back into the wagon and gave a happy sigh of relief.

"If you say so, Claude," she said.

CHAPTER

3

For the next few days Shirley and Claude headed
east in that great state called Texas. The dusty trail
rose and took them into land that was strewn with
rocks and boulders of all sizes.

Claude pulled the stumbling, but good-natured,
horses to a stop and said, "Shirley, I do believe this is
the peaceful place we've been lookin' for."

Shirley gazed out at the ridges and rocks and the
stubby trees whose roots clung to the patches of soil.
And she said, "I hope not, Claude. This land is
nothin' but bumpy-lumpy and makes me feel dry
enough to spit cotton."

"Never mind. This place will grow on you,
Shirley," Claude said. "For now, why don't you set
things to right around here. I'll get our sleepin' pallets
out of the wagon and tend to the horses."

So Shirley unfolded her long legs, stuck her feet in her boots, hiked up her skirts, and climbed down from the wagon. She strung a line between the rim of the wagon and a branch of a nearby tree, and on it she hung out to air Claude's long johns and his other shirt, and her petticoats and second-best, store-bought dress.

She was just finishing this chore when she heard a crackle of a broken twig. She turned around to see a large, mangy wolf creeping closer and closer. His eyes were narrow slits, his ears were laid back, and he was up to no good.

Shirley grabbed the nearest thing at hand, the frying pan that was hanging on the back of the wagon, and she let fly at the wolf.

Shirley's aim never was very good, so the frying pan hit the clothesline instead, sweeping it down, just as the wolf leaped forward.

Unfortunately for the wolf, he dove right inside the skirt and on up through the bodice of Shirley's second-best, store-bought dress. His head poked out of the sweetheart neckline, and his front paws were pinned so he couldn't use them.

Well, he set up a snarling and a yelping, meanwhile bouncing around on his back legs and making a terrible racket.

Just as Claude came around the front of the wagon to see what was going on, that old wolf bounced and leaped right on past him, carrying on something awful.

Claude watched the wolf until he disappeared around a far boulder, then he thought on it for a moment.

"Shirley," he said, "get back in the wagon. I don't know why that pointy-nose lady has got her dander up, but I sure don't want any near neighbors that mean and noisy. We're gonna have to move on."

Shirley gathered up their things, put them into the back of the wagon, and climbed up on the seat next to Claude. She gave a happy sigh of relief and said, "If you say so, Claude."

CHAPTER

4

The trail into that great state called Texas curled
east and southeast into its heartland. And as it rose
it softened into rolling hills, with meadows cupped
between. Splashes of blue and gold and red
wildflowers dotted the grassy hillsides, and great
oaks spread their branches to make deep pools
of shade.

Upward they went, until they crested a gentle hill.

Shirley put a hand on Claude's arm and said,
"Stop the wagon, Claude."

He pulled the tired, but good-natured, horses
to a stop under a stand of oaks, and she said, "Take
a look around us. Breathe in that pure air. How's
this for a place of peace and quiet?"

"I don't know," Claude said. "Any place that looks
this good is bound to get filled up with people afore
long. And then we wouldn't remember what peace
and quiet were all about."

"Down at the foot of the hill is a stream, probably just jumpin' with fish," Shirley said. "And you can look far enough in both directions goin' and comin' so you could spot a traveler and think on him two days afore he got here."

"I don't know," Claude said again. "Get down from the wagon, Shirley, and see what you can put together for supper. I'll get our sleeping pallets out of the wagon and tend to the horses."

Shirley unfolded her long legs, stuck her feet in her boots, hiked up her skirts, and climbed down from the wagon. She took out the stew pot and set it on the ground under an old and gnarled oak tree. Then she took down the rifle. She was going into the woods to find some fresh meat for the table.

Suddenly she heard the rustle of small leaves, and she looked up to see a big bobcat on a branch near her head. His narrow eyes were gleaming, his lips were pulled back in a snarl, and his tail was twitching. Shirley knew he was getting his mind set to spring.

Well, Shirley stared that bobcat square in the eyes and said to him, "I've found my peaceful place, and you're not goin' to spoil it for me." She raised her rifle, aimed it dead center at the bobcat, and pulled the trigger.

Shirley's aim never was very good. The shot hit that old tree branch, snapping it with a crack that flipped the bobcat in an arc right over the wagon. He came down so hard against a boulder that the force knocked it loose, and it rolled down the hill, tearing up the turf.

Behind it came the screeching bobcat, all spraddle-legged, with every pointy claw digging furrows in the soil as he slid down the hill.

Splat! went the boulder into the stream, knocking two good-sized, unsuspecting trout up on the bank and damming up a nice little pond. The bobcat flew over the stream and ran off so fast that Shirley knew she'd seen the last of him.

Claude came running and said, "Shirley, what was makin' all that racket?"

"Nothin' much," Shirley said. "Just a few things gettin' done around here after a branch fell off that tree."

Claude peered at the tree. "Seems there's something oozin' out of that tree into our stew pot," he said.

"What pure good luck!" Shirley said. "Looks like when that branch broke, it opened a honey cache, Claude. You'll have somethin' good on your biscuits tonight."

She took his arm and pointed him toward the sloping hillside. "Take notice that my vegetable garden's already plowed, and there's two good-sized trout down by the stream that are goin' to be pan-fried for supper."

Claude thought on this a moment. Then he said, "Shirley, get back in the wagon and start pullin' out the stuff we'll need. If you can just learn to do your chores without makin' so much noise, then I think we've found us our place of peace and quiet."

Shirley leaned against the wagon and gave a happy sigh of relief. She looked down at the stream that was sparking with pieces of afternoon sunlight, and she gazed out over the hills and the meadows that were soft and pleasing to the eyes.

She gave Claude the biggest smile he'd ever seen anyone come up with, and she said, "If you say so, Claude."

T H E   E N D

MEET MY FRIENDS

SHIRLEY & CLAUDE

by Joan Lowery Nixon

Joan Lowery Nixon

The idea for *If You Say So, Claude* began with my decision to write a Texas tall tale. The setting of the story, of course, would be somewhere in Texas. Thirty years ago, when my husband told me that we were moving to Texas, all I could picture was the dry ranch land, dotted with cactus and scrub brush, that I'd seen in cowboy movies. But I found that the huge state of Texas has a wide variety of landscapes.

Just as shown in the cowboy movies, there *are* miles and miles of flat desert in west and south Texas. However, in north Texas there are rugged canyons, some of central Texas is rocky with buttes and boulders, east Texas is thick with piney woods and swamps, and the Gulf Coast of Texas gleams with sunlight on the ocean. But deep in the heart of Texas is the prize—the Texas hill country—with its oaks and elms, its clear streams and lakes, and its soft, rolling hills. In the springtime these hills are carpeted with the blue and red flowers of Texas bluebonnets and Indian paintbrush.

JULY 9

8 PM — 8 PM

ONE NIGHT ONLY!

⪢ Ms. Joan Lowery Nixon ⪡

MAKING A SCHEDULED STOP AT THE

San Antonio Opera House

READING FROM HER TALL TALE

IF YOU SAY SO, CLAUDE

25¢ — **ADMISSION** — 25¢

What would my Texas tall tale be about? My son-in-law had been complaining about the heavy traffic in Houston and wishing he could find "a peaceful place to live." So I thought about someone who might come to Texas, desperately looking for a peaceful place. He'd have to be escaping a noisy place, and what could be noisier than one of the busy Colorado mining towns?

He probably wouldn't want to travel alone, so I gave him a wife. Shirley popped into my mind, name and all. She had courage and spunk, a good sense of humor, and a great smile. Was there anything Shirley couldn't do? As a matter of fact, yes. To begin with, Shirley wasn't very good with a rifle, and there were a few other things she found difficult—like baking an apple pie. I liked Shirley so much I didn't mind her few faults, and I didn't think her husband would either.

Since Shirley was tall and skinny, I thought her husband should be short and chubby. I'd give him a scraggly, gray beard that waggled when he talked. I had to search for exactly the right name for him, and I used a book called *What to Name Your Baby*. I read through all the names beginning with A and B, but it wasn't until I was in the C's that I found just what I wanted: Claude. Shirley and Claude, Shirley and Claude. Said together, their names had a nice rhythm.

I enjoyed writing about Shirley and Claude, and they became my friends. After putting them through a great deal of trouble looking for their peaceful place, I rewarded them with a home in the beautiful Texas hill country.

But soon I broke the news to them. Their life in the hill country wouldn't be quite as peaceful as they'd hoped because I wanted to involve them in other adventures. Would they mind?

Claude thought on it a moment, and then he grumbled, "Well . . . I guess I can't object. We'll do it."

But Shirley gave me such a big smile it lit up all the dark and dusty corners in my office. She winked at me, then turned to her husband. "If you say so, Claude," she said.

Pulling It All Together

1. If Claude and Shirley came to your neighborhood, would they say, "I do believe this is the peaceful place we've been lookin' for"? Why?
2. Climb a mountain! Read a hundred books! Get on base in every baseball game. What challenge will you choose? Which three characters from this book will you choose to help you? Why will you choose them?
3. The stories, poems, and articles in this book are about challenges. What other challenges would you like to read about? How can you find these things to read?

Books to Enjoy

Storm in the Night
by Mary Stolz
Illustrations by Pat Cummings

Sitting without lights through a fearsome thunderstorm, Grandfather tells Thomas a story about a storm that happened when he was a boy.

The Big Balloon Race
by Eleanor Coerr

Ariel falls asleep in her mother's hot-air balloon and flies in an important balloon race. Will she put aside her fears to help her mother win this race?

Grandma's Secret
by Paulette Bourgeois
Illustrations by Maryann Kovalski

A mysterious secret looms beyond Grandma's basement door. Grandma says it's a bear! Her grandson must walk down those dark steps to find out what makes that noise in the cellar.

A Picture Book of Martin Luther King, Jr.

by David A. Adler
Illustrations by Robert Casilla

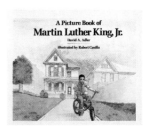

Martin Luther King, Jr., took on a big challenge in his lifetime. He wanted to see all people living together in peace.

The Ghost-Eye Tree

by Bill Martin, Jr., and John Archambault
Illustrations by Ted Rand

On a dark and windy autumn night, a brother and sister must walk to the end of town, past the dreaded ghost-eye tree, to get milk at the dairy.

Finding a Way: Living with Exceptional Brothers and Sisters

by Maxine B. Rosenberg
Photographs by George Ancona

Three young people talk about the challenges and the pleasures in living with brothers or sisters who have special needs.

Vinegar Pancakes and Vanishing Cream

by Bonnie Pryor

Living with a name like Martin Elwood Snodgrass is challenging enough, but having a family as successful as his makes Martin's life even more challenging.

Literary Terms

Characters

You can tell a lot about **characters** by the way they act. Claude is easily fooled. He decides the rabbit is shooting back at Shirley and thinks the wolf in Shirley's dress is a "pointy-nosed lady," so he wants to keep going on the trail through Texas. Shirley is smart. When she sees the hill country with oak trees and flowers, she wants that to be home. What does Shirley do to make sure Claude likes it too?

Fable

A **fable** is a short story that teaches a lesson. Usually, the characters in a fable are animals. "The Tiger and the Fox" is a Chinese fable that tells how important it is to use your brain. "Using Your Head," a fable from India, teaches the same lesson. "Doctor Coyote" and "The Fox and the Goat" also teach lessons about using your head. Fables come from all parts of the world, but the lessons are often the same.

Fantasy

In **fantasy,** an author creates a story about something that could not happen. One kind of fantasy is a ghost story. In *The Boy and the Ghost* most things seem real but, of course, the ghost is not real. Some people believe that imaginary ghosts like the one in the story watch over hidden treasure and that they are good to people who are not afraid of them. Did you think Thomas was brave when he offered the ghost some of his soup?

Setting

In some stories, the **setting** is very important. Sometimes the story could not take place anywhere else. *Chin Chiang and the Dragon's Dance* is one of those stories. Why does this story happen in Chinatown? What do the pictures tell you about the neighborhood?

Tall Tale

A **tall tale** is a story with characters who solve problems by performing humorous, almost superhuman, deeds. Tall tales celebrate the spirit of the people who built our country. Each time Shirley tries to get food for supper, something wild happens. The crazy, exaggerated things that happen make tall tales fun to read.

Glossary

Words from your stories

a·bide (ə bīd′), to put up with; endure: *I can't abide people who are always late.* verb, **a·bides, a·bid·ed, a·bid·ing.**
abide by, to accept and carry out; obey: *Both teams will abide by the umpire's decision.*

aim (ām), **1** to point or direct something in order to hit: *Molly aimed carefully at the target.* **2** the act of pointing or directing at something: *She hit the target because her aim was good.* **3** to direct words or acts so as to influence a certain person or action: *The teacher's talk was aimed at the students who cheated on the test.* **4** to try: *He aimed to please his teachers.* 1,3,4 *verb,* 2 *noun.*

a·shamed (ə shāmd′), **1** feeling shame; disturbed or uncomfortable because one has done something wrong, bad, or silly: *I was ashamed of the lies I had told.* **2** unwilling because of fear of shame: *I was ashamed to tell my parents I had failed math. adjective.*

av·er·age (av′ər ij), **1** the usual sort or amount: *The amount of rain this year has been below average.* **2** usual; ordinary: *The average teenager likes rock music.* 1 *noun,* 2 *adjective.*

beard (bird), **1** the hair growing on a man's chin and cheeks: *Grandpa shaved off his beard for the hot summer months.* **2** something like this. The long hair on the chin of a goat is a beard; so are the stiff hairs on the heads of plants like oats, barley, and wheat. *noun.*

bold (bōld), **1** without fear; having or showing courage; brave: *The bold knight went out to fight the fierce dragon.* **2** rude; impudent: *The bold child made faces at us as we passed.* **3** sharp and clear to the eye; striking: *The mountains stood in bold outline against the sky. adjective.*

beard
The man's beard was very thick.

a hat	i it	oi oil	ch child	ə stands for:
ā age	ī ice	ou out	ng long	a in about
ä far	o hot	u cup	sh she	e in taken
e let	ō open	u̇ put	th thin	i in pencil
ē equal	ô order	ü rule	ᴛʜ then	o in lemon
ėr term			zh measure	u in circus

bore (bôr), **1** to make weary by being uninteresting: *How can you stand that boring television show?* **2** a dull, tiresome person or thing: *It is a bore to wash dishes.* **1** *verb,* **bores, bored, bor·ing;** **2** *noun.*

broad (brôd), **1** wide; large across: *The broad new highway has six lanes.* **2** large; not limited or narrow; of wide range: *Our teacher has had broad experience with children.* **3** clear; full: *The theft was made in broad daylight.* *adjective.*

bul·ly (bu̇l′ē), **1** a person who teases, threatens, or hurts smaller or weaker people: *The bullies made the younger children on the school bus give up their seats.* **2** to frighten into doing something: *Stop trying to bully me into doing what you want.* **1** *noun, plural* **bul·lies;** **2** *verb,* **bul·lies, bul·lied, bul·ly·ing.**

clam·or (klam′ər), **1** a loud noise, especially of voices; continuous uproar: *The clamor of the crowd filled the air.* **2** to make a loud noise or continuous uproar: *The children were clamoring for candy.* **1** *noun,* **2** *verb.*

clump (klump), **1** a number of things of the same kind growing or grouped together; cluster: *I hid in a clump of trees.* **2** to walk in a heavy, clumsy, noisy manner: *The hiker clumped along in heavy boots.* **1** *noun,* **2** *verb.*

clum·sy (klum′zē), **1** awkward in moving: *The heavy cast on my broken leg made me clumsy.* **2** not well-shaped or well-made: *Our boat was a clumsy thing made out of scrap wood.* *adjective.* **clum·si·er, clum·si·est.**

cool (kül), **1** somewhat cold; more cold than hot: *a cool day.* **2** not excited; calm: *Everyone kept cool when paper in the wastebasket caught fire.* **3** very good; excellent: *That movie was so cool that it was worth seeing twice.* *adjective.*

cour·age (kėr′ij), bravery; meeting danger without fear: *It takes courage for many students to read aloud in class.* *noun.*

clump (def. 1)
A clump of trees grew along the shore.

dan·ger (dān/jər), **1** a chance of harm; nearness to harm; risk; peril: *The trip through the jungle was full of danger.* **2** a thing that may cause harm: *Hidden rocks are a danger to ships. noun.*

de·spair (di sper/ *or* di spar/), the loss of hope; a dreadful feeling that nothing good can happen to you: *We were filled with despair as we felt the boat slowly sinking. noun.*

dwarf (dwôrf), **1** a person, animal, or plant much smaller than the usual size for its kind: *Tom's brother Mark is a dwarf, so Tom made him a special-sized table and chair.* **2** in fairy tales, an ugly little man with magic power. **3** to cause to seem small by contrast or by distance. **1,2** *noun, plural* **dwarfs, dwarves** (dwôrvz); **3** *verb.*

examine (def. 1)

ex·am·ine (eg zam/ən), **1** to look at closely and carefully: *The doctor examined the people who had been hurt in the crash.* **2** to test; test the knowledge or ability of; ask questions of: *The lawyer examined the witness. verb.* **ex·am·ines, ex·am·ined, ex·am·in·ing.**

fa·mil·iar (fə mil/yər), **1** well-known; common: *Elena saw many familiar faces at the party.* **2** having a good or thorough knowledge of: *She is familiar with French and English. adjective.*

fat·ten (fat/n), **1** to make fat: *The farmer will fatten up the pigs before he sells them.* **2** to become fat: *The pigs fattened on corn. verb.*

gen·er·ous (jen/ər əs), **1** willing to share with others; unselfish: *Our teacher is always generous with his time.* **2** large; plentiful: *A quarter of a pie is a generous piece. adjective.*

ghost (gōst), the spirit of one who is dead appearing to the living: *The fairy tale was about a ghost who made friends with living people. noun.*

a hat	i it	oi oil	ch child	ə stands for:
ā age	ī ice	ou out	ng long	a in about
ä far	o hot	u cup	sh she	e in taken
e let	ō open	u̇ put	th thin	i in pencil
ē equal	ô order	ü rule	ᴛʜ then	o in lemon
ėr term			zh measure	u in circus

ghost·ly (gōst′lē), like a ghost; pale, dim, and shadowy: *A ghostly form walked across the stage. adjective,* **ghost·li·er, ghost·li·est.**

good-na·tured (gu̇d′nā′chərd), pleasant; kindly; obliging; cheerful: *The police officer is popular because he is helpful and good-natured. adjective.*

haunt·ed (hôn′tid), visited by ghosts: *They were afraid to go into the haunted house. adjective.*

haunted
The old house at the top of the hill looked haunted.

hon·est (on′ist), **1** fair and upright; truthful; not lying, cheating, or stealing: *The storekeeper is honest and always gives the correct change.* **2** not hiding one's real nature; frank; open: *She is honest about her feelings. adjective.*

ig·nore (ig nôr′), to pay no attention to; disregard: *The driver ignored the traffic light and almost hit another car. verb,* **ig·nores, ig·nored, ig·nor·ing.**

joint (joint), **1** the place at which two things or parts are joined together. A pocketknife has a joint to fold the blade inside the handle. **2** the place in an animal skeleton where two bones join. There is usually motion at a joint: *Grandma's joints hurt when the weather is damp.* **3** sharing: *My sister and I are joint owners of this dog.* **1,2** *noun,* **3** *adjective.*
out of joint, moved out of place at the joint: *The fall put his shoulder out of joint.*

limb (lim), **1** a leg, arm, or wing: *All of my limbs felt weak after the swimming race.* **2** a large branch: *They sawed the dead limb off the tree. noun.*

mange (mānj), a skin disease of both animals and humans that causes scabs and loss of hair: *One of the squirrels at our feeder seems to have mange. noun.*

141

mangy (mān′jē), **1** having the characteristics of mange: *We took the mangy dog to the vet to be treated and bathed.* **2** mean or shabby: *That was a mangy trick you played on Mike.* *adjective.* **mang·i·er, mang·i·est.** See **mange.**

pal·let (pal′it), a bed of straw; poor bed: *The campers laid out their sleeping bags on pallets in the cabin.* noun.

po·lite (pə līt′), behaving properly; having or showing good manners: *The polite girl gave the old man her seat on the bus.* *adjective,* **po·lit·er, po·lit·est.**

prey (prā), **1** an animal hunted or seized for food: *Mice and birds are the prey of cats.* **2** the habit of hunting and killing other animals for food: *Hawks are birds of prey.* *noun, plural* **prey.**
prey on or **prey upon, 1** to hunt or kill for food: *Cats prey upon mice.* **2** to do harm; be a strain upon: *Worry about debts preyed on her mind.*

proud (proud), having pleasure or satisfaction in oneself or one's achievements: *I am proud to have been chosen class president.* *adjective.*
proud of, thinking well of; being well satisfied with: *to be proud of oneself, to be proud of one's family.*

rack·et (rak′it), **1** a loud noise; din; loud talk: *Don't make a racket when others are reading.* **2** a dishonest scheme for getting money from people, often by threatening to hurt them or what belongs to them. *noun.*

re·lax (ri laks′), **1** to loosen up; make or become less stiff or firm: *Relax your muscles to rest them. Relax when you dance.* **2** to make or become less strict or severe; lessen in force: *Discipline is relaxed on the last day of school.* **3** to relieve or be relieved from work, effort, or worry: *We relaxed during the holidays.* *verb.*

slith·er (sliᴛʜ′ər), to go with a sliding motion: *The snake slithered into the weeds.* *verb.*

slither

a hat	i it	oi oil	ch child	ə stands for:
ā age	ī ice	ou out	ng long	a in about
ä far	o hot	u cup	sh she	e in taken
e let	ō open	ù put	th thin	i in pencil
ē equal	ô order	ü rule	ᴛʜ then	o in lemon
ėr term			zh measure	u in circus

slith·er·y (sliᴛʜ′ər ē). See **slither.** *adjective.*

spook·y (spü′kē), strange and frightening; suggesting the presence of ghosts: *The old house looked spooky.* *adjective,* **spook·i·er, spook·i·est.**

stalk (stôk), **1** to hunt by following silently and carefully: *The hungry lion stalked a zebra.* **2** to walk in a slow, stiff, or proud manner: *She stalked into the room and threw herself into a chair.* *verb.*

ter·ri·fy (ter′ə fī), to fill with great fear; frighten very much: *The loud, violent storm terrified the hikers. verb,* **ter·ri·fies, ter·ri·fied, ter·ri·fy·ing.**

treas·ure (trezh′ər), **1** wealth or riches stored up; valuable things: *The pirates buried treasure along the coast.* **2** any thing or person that is much loved or valued: *The silver teapot was my parents' chief treasure.* **3** to value highly: *She treasures her train more than all her other toys.* **1,2** *noun,* **3** *verb,* **treas·ures, treas·ured, treas·ur·ing.**

wealth (welth), **1** riches; many valuable possessions; property: *The family used its wealth to build a hospital.* **2** a large quantity; abundance: *a wealth of hair, a wealth of words. noun.*

wit (wit), **1** the power to perceive quickly and express cleverly ideas that are unusual, striking, and amusing: *Her wit even made her troubles seem amusing.* **2** understanding; mind; sense: *People with quick wits learn easily. noun.*

treasure (def. 1)

Acknowledgments

Text

Pages 6–23: Reprinted by permission of Margaret K. McElderry Books, an imprint of Macmillan Publishing Company, from *Chin Chiang and the Dragon's Dance* by Ian Wallace. Copyright © 1984 by Ian Wallace.

Pages 24–26: "Drum Up a Dragon" by Ian Wallace. Copyright © 1991 by Ian Wallace.

Pages 28–44: From *The Knight Who Was Afraid of the Dark* by Barbara Shook Hazen, illustrated by Tony Ross. Text copyright © 1989 by Barbara Shook Hazen. Illustration copyright © 1989 by Tony Ross. Reprinted by permission of Dial Books for Young Readers.

Pages 48–49: "Using Your Head" from *Jataka Tales* by Nancy DeRoin, pp. 27–28. Text copyright © 1975 by Nancy DeRoin. Reprinted by permission of Houghton Mifflin Company.

Pages 50–51: Excerpts and illustrations from *A Chinese Zoo.* Copyright © 1987 by Demi. Reprinted by permission of Harcourt Brace Jovanovich, Inc.

Pages 52–53: "The Fox and the Goat" from *Aesop's Fables,* retold by Anne Terry White, illustrated by Helen Siegel. Copyright © 1964 by Anne Terry White. Reprinted by permission of Random House, Inc.

Pages 54–56: from *Doctor Coyote: A Native American Aesop's Fables,* retold by John Bierhorst and illustrated by Wendy Watson. Text copyright © 1987 by John Bierhorst. Illustrations copyright © 1987 by Wendy Watson. Reprinted by permission of Macmillan Publishing Company.

Pages 58–66: *City Mouse and Country Mouse* by Jane Buxton. First published in the *New Zealand School Journal,* Part 2, Number 2, 1988. Copyright © 1988 by Jane Buxton. Reprinted by permission of the author.

Page 68: "Manhattan Lullabye" by Norma Farber. Copyright Thomas Farber. Reprinted by permission of Thomas Farber.

Page 69: "Country Road, Spring Walk" from *Country Pie* by Frank Asch. Copyright © 1979 by Frank Asch. Reprinted by permission of Greenwillow Books, a division of William Morrow & Company, Inc.

Pages 70–82: From *Thinking Big* by Susan Kuklin. Copyright © 1986 by Susan Kuklin. Reprinted by permission of Lothrop, Lee & Shepard Books, a division of William Morrow & Company, Inc.

Pages 84–104: From *The Boy and the Ghost* by Robert D. San Souci. Copyright © 1989 by Robert D. San Souci. Used by permission of the publisher, Simon and Schuster Books for Young Readers, New York, NY, 10020.

Pages 106–129: From *If You Say So, Claude* by Joan Lowery Nixon, illustrated by Lorinda Bryan Cauley. Copyright © 1980 by Joan Lowery Nixon, illustration © 1980 by Lorinda Bryan Cauley. Used by permission of Viking Penguin, a division of Penguin Books USA Inc.

Pages 130–132: "Meet My Friends Shirley and Claude" by Joan Lowery Nixon. Copyright © 1991 by Joan Lowery Nixon.

Artists

Illustrations owned and copyrighted by the illustrator.
Petra Mathers, cover, 1–5, 133, 136–137, 144
Sarah Frederking (calligraphy), cover, 1–5, 133, 134, 136, 138, 144
Ian Wallace, 6–23, 27
Tony Ross, 28–45
Mary Jones, 46–47
Paul Hoffman, 48–49
Demi, 50–51
Helen Siegel, 52
Wendy Watson, 54–57
Kate Brennan Hall, 58–67
Mary Lynn Blasutta, 68
David Cunningham, 69
J. Brian Pinkney, 84–105
Lorinda Bryan Cauley, 106–129
Paul Uhl, 131

Photographs

Unless otherwise acknowledged, all photographs are the property of Scott Foresman.
Pages 25 and 26: Courtesy of Ian Wallace
Pages 70–83: Photographs from *Thinking Big* by Susan Kuklin, copyright © 1986. Used by permission of William Morrow and Company, Inc. Publishers, New York.
Page 131: Courtesy of Joan Lowery Nixon
Page 138, 141: Dan Morrill
Page 139: James P. Rowan
Page 141: Michael Fogden/Oxford Scientific Films/*Animals, Animals*
Page 143: Culver Pictures, Inc.

Glossary

The contents of the Glossary have been adapted from *Beginning Dictionary,* Copyright © 1988, Scott, Foresman and Company.

144